CHRONICLES OF FAITH

ABRAHAM LINCOLN

Sam Wellman

Illustrated by
Ken Save

BARBOUR
PUBLISHING

CHRONICLES OF FAITH

ABRAHAM
LINCOLN

"Can I go explore now, Father?"

1

SHIRTTAIL BOY

"Can I go explore now, Father?" asked Abe.

Tom Lincoln stopped chopping wood with an ax and gave Abe a stern look. "If you've finished your chores, you can go play. But don't go down near the creek!"

Abe glanced down at Knob Creek. White water boiled over and around the rocks. He looked up a slope toward cliffs that shot straight up to the sky. The cliffs were dotted with stout cedar trees. Abe trudged up the slope.

Today another boy explored the slope above the log cabin where Abe lived. The boy wore yellow pants made from deer hide like Abe's father wore. Deer hide was called buckskin. The boy in buckskin put his fists on his hips and growled, "I'm Austin. What's your name, shirttail boy?"

"I'm Abe." All his life Abe had never worn pants at all. He wore a long itchy shirt that came to his knees. He never thought the shirt was unusual until now.

Austin squinted. "How come I've never seen you before? How old are you?"

"Thanks for asking." Abe loved to tell stories, and this was one of his favorites. "I was born one morning over on Rock Spring Farm. My sister, Sarah, woke up and saw Father standing by the bed. Mother was in a heap of bearskins on the bed. She was holding a wrinkly red baby in a blanket. Sarah said my eyes and fists were closed tighter than walnuts. Black hair already plastered my head. Mother said, 'Let's name this boy Abraham after your father, Tom. . . .'"

"How old are you?" asked Austin impatiently.

"I was born to Nancy and Tom Lincoln on the Lord's Day, February 12, in the year 1809. . . ."

6

"I'm Abe."

"This is 1814. You're only five? You're as big as me, and I'm seven. Can you wrestle, shirttail boy?" Austin's hands became spidery, ready to grab Abe.

"Like this?" Abe wrestled Austin to the ground. He let Austin get up right away. He knew when he wrestled Sarah she got real mad if he held her down very long.

Austin grinned. "Yes. Like that. When are you coming to school, Abe?"

"What do you do at school?"

"I learn reading and writing and ciphering. Ciphering is adding up and subtracting numbers."

Abe shrugged. "I know all twenty-six letters of the alphabet. I can count to a hundred. I can't go to school anyway. I have chores to do. I carry water. I fill the wood box. I hoe weeds. I slop the hogs. I poke seeds of corn into plowed

Abe wrestled Austin to the ground.

ground. I fetch tools for Father. . . ."

Austin interrupted him. "I get the idea. You're not coming to school."

And the boys played hide-and-seek in a field of corn.

A few days after Abe met Austin, Tom Lincoln hitched two horses to their big wagon. Tom lifted Abe into the wagon. Abe asked suspiciously, "Are you taking me to school?"

"No. We're going to Elizabethtown."

In Elizabethtown, Abe saw a man with black skin being worked like a mule. The man's eyes never left the ground. Tom explained the black man was a "slave" owned by the mill owner.

Abe noticed something. His father's voice was cheerful and light when he had been telling funny stories in front of the general store. Now his voice was sad and heavy—like

Abe saw a man with black skin
being worked like a mule.

the time they found their hog chewed up by a bear.

Abe asked, "How can a man own another man?"

Tom grunted. "It's the law here in Kentucky. All black folks in Kentucky are slaves."

Abe looked up and down the street. He saw lots of black folks—black women and children, too. "What law?"

"Rules white men make up."

"What's Kentucky?"

Tom had to laugh. "Elizabethtown here and the farm where we live are inside the state called Kentucky. There are seventeen other states in the United States. That's the nation we live in. Israel in the Good Book is a nation."

All the way home, Abe thought about laws and states and nations and slaves. Things were simple on their farm. Abe knew how to make

Abe thought about laws and states and
nations and slaves.

soap and candles. He saw how his mother ground corn into cornmeal, then baked it to make bread. He saw how his father, Tom, took rough walnut logs and made them into a smooth corner cabinet. But away from the farm, Abe knew almost nothing. How would he ever know these things?

Every Sunday the Lincolns walked to Little Mount Church. Preacher Elkin talked from the Good Book about the good news that Jesus had died and come alive again. But then the preacher closed the Good Book and frowned as he talked about how bad folks were who owned slaves.

When Abe or Sarah made the Lincolns late to church, Abe could sometimes hear Preacher Elkin preaching even though they were still a long way off. Preacher Elkin could talk softly, too. And Abe watched how the preacher used his arms. Once in awhile

The preacher talked about how bad folks
were who owned slaves.

the preacher would throw his arms high, rise right up on his toes, and boom his voice off the ceiling.

On the way home, Tom would say, "Mighty powerful preaching today. . ."

Mother would add, "No one can preach like Preacher Elkin."

One morning after a breakfast of eggs and bacon, Abe's mother said, "Abe has been shirttail boy long enough."

Tom didn't go outside to do chores like he usually did after breakfast. He grinned and said, "This I have to see."

"Here, Abe." Mother held up a pair of pants!

Abe fell down twice trying to get them on. Finally, he sat on a bench and tugged them on. The pants were made from yellow buckskin like Austin's. But Abe's pants were new and spotless. When he walked around in them, they felt stiff and very heavy. He felt

Mother held up a pair of pants!

like he was wading through water.

Mother said, "Put on your moccasins, Abe."

"Why? It didn't snow." Then he noticed Sarah was wearing a new dress. It was made of a kind of cotton cloth Mother called calico. Abe muttered, "What's going on?"

Tom said, "Let's get going. It's two miles away. I'll give you a ride the first day."

Abe asked, "What's two miles away?"

Sarah laughed. "School, fancy pants."

"It's a blab school," said Mother.

Abe rode in the wagon with Tom and Sarah to the rough cabin that was a school. Inside, Abe saw Austin jabbering out of a book. All twenty boys and girls sat on benches and jabbered lessons out loud at the same time so that the teacher would know they were working.

Abe blurted, "So that's why Mother calls it a blab school."

"What's going on?"

Abe already knew the alphabet. It wasn't long before he blabbed words from a thin book called a speller. After one month he blabbed from the speller a whole sentence of one-syllable words: "Trust in the Lord with all your heart."

His teacher said, "That's a proverb, right out of the Bible."

"My mother reads that same proverb out of the Good Book we have at home."

That fact hit Abe like a bolt of lightning! At home that night he began to read the Good Book. On the very first page it said the Good Book was God's greatest gift!

Every night the Lincolns sat together in front of the fireplace. While his mother read from the Bible, Abe studied her. She was thin and very tall. Dark brown hair was parted in the middle. Her face looked wrinkled and hollow. She was missing some teeth. She had

He began to read the Good Book.

a high forehead and yellow brown eyes. Long ago, when she was still called Nancy Hanks, his mother must have looked like Sarah.

And while his father told stories of every kind, Abe sized him up. Tom wasn't much taller than Mother. But his shoulders were wide and his arms thick. Abe wasn't like him that way. Abe was thin and gawky. When Abe peered at himself in a mud puddle, the only things that looked like they belonged on his father were his coarse black hair and deep-set gray eyes.

There were silent times by the fire, too. Mother sewed. Tom cleaned his carpenter tools. Abe and Sarah did spelling and grammar lessons from their speller. The speller used examples from the Bible. For Abe and Sarah, the Good Book was everywhere. God's Word was as basic to their lives as air. They never ate a meal before Tom said, "Fit and prepare us

There were silent times by the fire.

for humble service for Christ's sake. Amen."

Abe practiced writing, too. Paper was far too precious to use. If he was in front of the fire, he blackened words on firewood with a piece of charcoal. If he was outside the cabin, he fingered words in the dirt or mud or snow.

But sometimes he just had fun exploring with Austin.

One time Abe's father went on a trip for nearly a month. Wintry clouds had been scraping the cliff tops, and it had been raining hard for a week. One morning the sun shone again. So Abe explored along the banks of Knob Creek with Austin. The water in Knob Creek didn't boil around the rocks like it usually did. No rocks could be seen at all.

Abe said, "The water looks calm."

"The water only looks calm because it's so deep and muddy. It's swifter than it's ever

"The water looks calm."

been." Austin sounded scared. "Look. It cut into the bank and knocked that old birch tree over."

"The tree toppled right across Knob Creek!" yelled Abe. "It's a bridge!" He jumped up on the dark, scaly bark. "We can see what's over on the other side."

Austin cried, "You better not, Abe! You can't swim!"

Abe slipped! The last thing he saw before he thrashed into the creek was Austin's mouth drop open in horror.

Abe slipped!

"Oh, please save me, Jesus. . . ."

2

Close Calls

Icy water yanked Abe along like a hundred horses. He clawed weeds at the bank's edge as he swept by them.

He saw Austin running along the bank beside him. The creek rolled Abe over. Water rushed into his nose. Pain stung below his eyes and inside his forehead. He tried to scream. Water choked him. He kicked a rock with his toe. He was sinking. He prayed, "Oh, please save me, Jesus. . . ."

Abe beat his arms against the crushing water. His fingers touched something, and he grabbed at it.

He held something in his hands! If only he could pull himself to the bank. But he was too weak. He would never make it. He couldn't breathe. Everything was spinning and going black.

Something whacked him on the back. He gagged. The creek gushed from his throat. Again and again he gagged. His back hurt. His stomach ached. His throat burned.

"Wake up, Abe!" It was Austin's voice.

Abe opened his eyes. He was on the bank. A branch was by his face. He sputtered, "I. . . I. . .I'm alive."

Austin said, "It's a good thing you grabbed that branch so I could haul you in."

Abe shivered from more than cold. It was quite awhile before he said, "I came one branch from dying."

"It was more than a branch," said Austin. "It was like your mother always says: God has a plan for you, Abe."

Abe was silent. He wasn't sure Austin was right. Could a boy be so foolish he could actually defeat God's plan? It was something very important to think about.

30

"I. . .I. . .I'm alive."

Three weeks before Christmas, his father, Tom, returned from the trip. That first night back, while all four Lincolns warmed in front of a fire roaring in the fireplace, Tom said, "We're going to move to a new state called Indiana."

Mother explained, "Father and I decided we have to leave Kentucky. Our neighbors are buying more and more slaves. In Indiana no man can be made a slave."

Abe knew Indiana must be someplace special.

Into the big wagon, they loaded everything they owned except their furniture. It was easier for Tom to make new furniture at their new home. Two horses pulled the wagon. Tied behind the wagon were two more horses and one cow. Three hounds chased each other around the wagon.

Abe was scared and shivering when he

"We're moving to a new state called Indiana."

climbed up into the wagon box. But he didn't complain. Tom turned on the wagon seat to say, "I'm sorry you children are cold. But winter is the best time to move. We're living off food we salted and dried anyway. And these roads are frozen as solid as rock instead of being knee-deep in mud."

They clopped along the frozen mud road mile after mile. Chickens clucked in wooden cages, and hogs grunted right next to Abe. He was sad as he remembered all the times he and Austin played together. Would he ever see Austin again?

The wagon stopped.

"I never saw such a thing!" shouted Sarah.

The gleaming ribbon of water was ten times wider than Abe could skip a flat rock. Tom laughed. "Only the men on the barges, flatboats, and big steamboats know how many times deeper than Abe's nose that Ohio River is."

"I never saw such a thing!"

Mother beamed. "On the other side is Indiana."

A ferryboat took them across the Ohio River, and they headed the wagon into woods folks called "rough." Indiana had rough like Abe had never seen before. Oak, sycamore, hackberry, ash, poplar, maple, and beech trees towered into the sky. Grapevines as thick as small trees webbed all the trees and undergrowth together.

"A snake has to work hard to squeeze through this rough," Tom joked. But he had to hack and chop from dawn to dusk, day after day, to clear the way for the wagon.

Tom seemed to relax after they reached a high area. He said, "This land is just above Little Pigeon Creek."

"Look. A half-face." Abe pointed at a crude three-sided lean-to called a half-faced camp. Three walls were made of logs and

"On the other side is Indiana."

boughs. The fourth side was open. "Someone lives here," said Abe.

"I built that." Tom waved around them. "This is the land I claimed."

Abe jumped out of the wagon. "So this is where you were while you were gone."

Tom nodded. "I stacked brush on each corner to mark our claim. The corners mark a square one-half mile on each side. Our land is rich in oak and hickory trees. Natural salt licks attract all kinds of wild critters. Springs seep good water north of the half-face. Over yonder to the east, there's a small stream moseying right across our land."

The three hounds were already learning the new property. Abe heard them way off somewhere in the tangled rough, baying and yelping.

Tom smiled. "Within one year, I have to ride up to the town of Vincennes. I have to

"So this is where you were."

pay eighty dollars to the government to get a paper that proves we own this one hundred sixty acres." He frowned. "We'll still owe them two hundred and forty dollars."

Abe whistled. "This land costs two whole dollars per acre!"

Mother said, "Let's get settled. Abe, unload a bag of cornmeal and a ham for supper. Sarah, spread leaves over the ground in the half-face."

Tom grabbed his ax. "I'll take care of the animals."

Tom built a shelter and corral for the horses and the cow. The sky was dark as he finished a separate one for the hogs. He saw Abe had moved the cages full of chickens into the half-face. A big fire had to be kept blazing there all the time in place of a fourth wall.

Tom said, "We'll build a chicken coop tomorrow. Then we'll start a cabin. We have two sharp axes."

"We'll still owe them two hundred
and forty dollars."

Two axes! It was the first night Abe didn't fall asleep thinking how much he missed Austin. Under wool blankets and bearskins, with hens clucking softly by his head, Abe dreamed of swinging the ax. Sometime in the night the hounds returned, panting and exhausted.

The next morning Tom said, "Let's get started." He handed seven-year-old Abe an ax.

Tom chopped down trees one foot thick that could be cut into logs twenty feet long. They needed thirty-two of these logs, eight for each wall. Abe whacked off the limbs. He notched the ends, so the logs would lock together.

They cut shorter logs for the gables, the uppermost triangle-shaped parts of the walls at each end of the cabin. They made a nice sloping roof by overlapping wood shingles on

"Let's get started."

thin logs that stretched from gable to gable. Inside the cabin, Tom placed beams from wall to wall eight feet above the floor. He pounded stout wood pegs up one wall.

Abe asked, "Why do you need those pegs?"

"You and Sarah will need them."

Abe shrugged. "What for?"

Tom laughed. "To climb up to the loft I'm going to build on the beams. That's where you and Sarah will sleep."

Abe and Sarah "chinked" thin slabs of wood in the cracks between the logs. After chinking, they daubed mud between the logs. To Abe the cabin was wonderful. His family made it right out of the forest. It was solid and safe and smelled of fresh cut wood.

Abe bragged, "We made the cabin in just four days."

"With God's mercy," said Mother.

"You handle an ax like a man, Abe." Tom

To Abe the cabin was wonderful.

looked puzzled, just like the time Mother convinced him Abe was really reading the Bible and not reciting it from memory.

Sarah scanned the thick rough woods around the cabin. "When are we going back to school?"

Tom said, "Folks can't get a teacher to come here yet. You can school yourself."

Abe practiced reading and writing every evening. A neighbor told Tom he wanted to write his mother in Kentucky but didn't know how to write. Tom told him maybe Abe could write a letter for him. So Abe not only wrote the letter but also worked out the very best way to write what the neighbor wanted to say. Soon other neighbors asked Abe to write letters for them. Tom heard folks at Gentry's store talking about how Abe was ahead of other boys his age. He was taller. He could write. And how he could swing an ax!

"You can school yourself."

Before the next winter, Abe's aunt and uncle, the Sparrows, and their son, Dennis Hanks, moved from Kentucky to live near the Lincolns. Although Dennis was several years older than Abraham, the two cousins became friends. When they found time, seventeen-year-old Dennis and Abe talked as equals: Dennis, an older fun-loving joker, and Abe, a younger "wizard" folks talked about.

Tom Lincoln got a copy of *Aesop's Fables*. Abe read it through and through. The fables weren't as deep and moving as the parables Jesus told in the Bible, but a fable about a fox and grapes was fun to read. Abe loved how fables and parables helped him understand life better. He turned stories inside and out, up and down, front and back. None of the Lincolns got much sleep any night. Abe kept talking about what a fable or a parable meant.

Abe kept talking about what a parable meant.

"Jumping Jehoshaphat," exclaimed Tom. "I never saw anyone chew on an idea like you. You're like an Indian woman chewing deer hide until it's soft. You won't let go of it until you've got it exactly the way it's supposed to be."

Mother added, "The only time Abe loses his temper is when he doesn't understand something he reads or hears."

Once in awhile now, Abe got to ride a horse alone to the mill. He took a bag of corn to grind into flour. The mill was the kind where the customer had to use his own horse to grind the corn. Abe hitched his horse to the beam and began strolling behind the horse on its endless circular path. It seemed like it would take forever.

"Get up, you old horse!" he yelled without thinking.

The frightened horse whinnied.

As quickly as a flick of the horse's tail, everything went black for Abe.

Everything went black for Abe.

"I can't get a pulse!"

3

MILK FEVER!

Abe drifted through space too black and too deep to ever put into words.

He heard a man cry, "I can't get a pulse! The poor boy is dead."

Abe opened his eyes. He was looking at the sky. Where was the horse? He felt the pebbly ground poking in his back.

A whiskery face looked down at him. "Abe's alive!" The face belonged to the owner of the mill.

Abe asked, "What happened, Mr. Gordon?"

Mr. Gordon pressed a wet rag against Abe's forehead. "You just lie down for a spell. Your horse almost kicked your head off, Abe." He whispered to someone. "I was sure Abe was dead."

After awhile Abe got up. A huge lump on his forehead throbbed pain with every heartbeat. As he rode the horse home, he recited verses memorized from the Bible. His mind worked all right. He didn't like to think about what had happened. That was the second time he almost died.

Tom Lincoln got Abe and Sarah a copy of *The Pilgrim's Progress*. Abe read *The Pilgrim's Progress* again and again just like other books. It told of a pilgrim's journey to save his soul from hell. The pilgrim survived one disaster after another and succeeded despite constant danger. Abe's own life on the frontier didn't always seem dangerous. That made it even more dangerous. One careless moment could end his life. He remembered the horse at the mill.

At the front of the book was a sketch of the life of the Englishman who wrote the book. Abe read that John Bunyan was "raised from the deepest obscurity. . .to be uncommonly

He recited verses memorized from the Bible.

useful for mankind." Every time Abe read that passage his heart was pounding so hard he had to stop.

He prayed, *How could anyone be more obscure than I am out here in the woods? Maybe I, too, can be uncommonly useful. Is that Your plan for me, God?*

Yet he knew how Bunyan's pilgrim suffered one disaster after another. Was that God's plan for him? Things were very pleasant right now on their farm. Every night he talked with his family and read in front of the fire. And he heard folks found a teacher. Abe might even get some schooling once in awhile.

Abe loved his job in the forest. Someday corn would stretch far beyond their cabin. Abe's job was to chop out bushes and grapevines growing under the trees. Tom was always within shouting distance, but Abe felt like he worked alone. He knew other folks were working just like him all around the forest. He imagined how they all cleared land

Abe loved his job in the forest.

farther and farther away from their cabins. Would the day ever come when they would all break out of the forest suddenly and he would see neighbors standing everywhere?

Abe never felt alone. The forest chattered and squeaked and bellowed with critters. It was a rare day a flock of passenger pigeons didn't darken the sky. Squirrels scolded him from the trees. Skunks ambled by fearlessly, armed with stinging smell. Wildcats hissed but were never seen. Blue-skinned lizards darted away. Snakes slithered under leaves. Wasps buzzed at him from papery nests.

Raccoons burst like fat fur balls from undergrowth to scurry up a tree. All day long Abe saw possums, groundhogs, badgers, mink, deer, foxes, toads, turkeys, ducks, and a hundred kinds of insects he couldn't name. The critters rustled, chattered, cheeped, and grunted all around him.

"Jumping Jehoshaphat!" he mimicked his

"Jumping Jehoshaphat!"

father. "How you critters can carry on."

The second summer in Indiana was not like the first summer. Tom grumbled, "It's too hot. It's too dry. I don't like this. Hot, dry summers are not good."

Abe said, "It's not so bad if you go swimming now and again." Abe heard about the local swimming hole on Little Pigeon Creek from Dennis Hanks. Abe was always hinting that he should be allowed to go there, too.

Abe's mother and father exchanged worried looks. Abe thought they worried about him swimming.

One late summer evening, Tom was too quiet by the fire. His face so darkened by the sun looked white. Finally he said, "I think our old cow has got the trembles."

"Trembles!" Mother, who was always calm, had to calm herself before she asked, "Are you sure she isn't just old?"

"I think our old cow has got the trembles."

Tom replied softly, "We'll wait and see. Nobody drink any milk or eat any cheese. Go to bed, children."

And Tom left the cabin for awhile.

Abe and Sarah climbed into the loft. Abe asked Sarah when she last drank milk. She couldn't remember. And he asked her when she last ate cheese. She wasn't sure when. Abe's mouth felt thick and cottony. He didn't like the taste of milk. He wasn't much of an eater at all. But he tried to remember: When did he last drink milk? When did he last eat cheese?

Lying up in the loft that night, Abe heard his father come back. Tom told Mother he had warned neighbors. Tom said in a worried whisper that because of the dry summer, the old cow had grazed far back into the woods. Two days later the cow died.

Tom sat the children down. "It's certain

When did he last drink milk?

now. Our old cow had the milk fever. Cows get it in hot, dry summers. The disease doesn't stop at the cow. Somehow it poisons the cow's milk. Somehow it poisons some folks who drink the cow's milk or eat cheese made from the cow's milk."

Dennis Hanks pounded on the door next morning. He was sobbing. "Mr. Sparrow woke up with a white tongue!"

Abe never heard such fear in Dennis before.

Mother gasped. "A white coating on the tongue is the first sure sign of milk fever!" And she rushed to help Mrs. Sparrow nurse Mr. Sparrow. When she came back that evening, she said grimly, "His stomach is burning—the second sure sign. He made out a will!"

Tom said, "Let us pray there is no third sign: a brown tongue."

The next day Mrs. Sparrow got a white tongue! Mr. Sparrow's tongue did turn brown,

"Mr. Sparrow woke up with a white tongue!"

and he died. In a daze, Mrs. Sparrow realized she would likely follow her husband. Abe's mother nursed her. Sarah helped.

Abe helped his father saw planks of black cherry wood. Then Tom planed them smooth. Abe whittled pegs. The pegs would hold on the lid of the coffin. Mr. Sparrow's coffin was as fine as Tom could make it in such a short time. Tom didn't say anything, but Abe knew he had started a second coffin for Mrs. Sparrow. And there were graves to dig deep into the yellow Indiana soil.

One morning when Nancy came back to the cabin, Tom asked her, "How is Mrs. Sparrow?"

Nancy winced as she sat down. "She's still alive, but not for long. She'll be gone by afternoon or evening."

Tom said, "Rest awhile before you go back."

Abe couldn't remember seeing his mother

"She'll be gone by afternoon or evening."

so tired. She had been tired a lot since coming to Indiana, but today she looked old, too. She seemed far older than thirty-four.

Mother said, "I won't be going back, Tom."

Fear erupted inside Abe as if he had just heard a thousand rattlesnakes all around him.

He cried, "Mother has milk fever!"

Abe's life seemed to come to a stop. Mother was lying in bed, her face chalk white. He prayed and prayed for her life to be spared. But she got the second sign, then the third. Life no longer made any sense to Abe.

Mother was calm. She smiled at Abe and Sarah. "We will be parting soon. This is a very sad time. But we cannot always understand our heavenly Father's ways. You children won't think so, but I'm lucky. It won't be long until I see our Savior, Jesus."

Abe was nine years old when Nancy Lincoln died. He and Sarah brooded for their mother. And what if their father got milk fever?

Abe was nine years old when Nancy Lincoln died.

Days after Mother was buried on a knoll in sight of the cabin, Tom took Abe and Sarah by the hand and marched them down the familiar trail to Jim Gentry's store. Then he turned and walked them down a strange trail. It took them one hour to reach a flat-roofed cabin.

Tom said, "You children must go on with your lives."

Abe heard a chorus of voices. Tom opened the door and nudged Abe and Sarah inside. Heads of children turned to gawk at them. The room fell into silence.

Tom handed a man something wrapped in cloth. Tom said, "These children are Sarah and Abe Lincoln."

And the man said, "Howdy-do! I'm Andrew Crawford. Thanks kindly for the bacon. Sit down, Sarah and Abe. Take off that coonskin cap, Abe."

Tom Lincoln turned and left.

"Howdy-do! I'm Andrew Crawford."

Andrew Crawford taught a blab school. But he spent the whole morning on manners. Pupils practiced saying a cheerful "howdy-do!" When a boy entered a room, he took off his cap. Outside, boys tipped their caps and introduced themselves. Girls curtsied. Boys and girls both practiced opening doors for older folks.

Abe ate his lunch of corn dodgers and dried apples next to a boy who was older but about Abe's size.

The boy said, "Howdy-do, Abe. I'm Matt Gentry."

"Your father must run the general store."

"Yes, he does. Isn't your father the carpenter?"

Abe was stunned. He thought of his father, Tom, as a farmer. Matt called his father a carpenter, a man who made things of wood. That made Abe the "carpenter's son." He had read those very words in the Good Book a hundred times. It took his breath away.

"Isn't your father the carpenter?"

Would they spend Christmas alone?

4

GOD'S PLAN

Of course, Abe knew the "carpenter's son," Jesus, was really the Son of God. Abe was only a boy. Still, he wanted to believe it was a sign from God that he might amount to something.

The next year was rough on twelve-year-old Sarah. She worked hard to do all the work her mother had done in the cabin and garden. Abe and Tom helped but weren't as particular as Sarah. And besides, they had work in the fields and forest to do.

One month before Christmas, Tom said, "Children, I have to go on a trip." And Tom rode off on a horse without another word of explanation.

Abe was only ten. He had never felt more hopeless. He acted cheerful for Sarah. Every night he prayed for his father to return.

Would they spend Christmas alone?

What if his father never came back at all?

A few days before Christmas, Abe and Sarah were inside the cabin when they heard a wagon rattling up the trail.

"Maybe it's Father!" yelled Sarah.

"He didn't take a wagon," reasoned Abe glumly, but he ran out of the cabin with Sarah. He couldn't give up hope.

Off the wagon jumped a boy about half as tall as Abe. He stuck out his chest. "I'm John. I'm seven."

A girl stepped down. "I'm Elizabeth. I'm nine." She pointed at a young girl clinging to the wagon. "That's Matilda. She's five."

Abe blurted, "Are you folks just passing through?"

Suddenly Tom stood there with a woman. He said, "This is Sally, your new mother. All the way from Elizabethtown."

Abe was flabbergasted. What could he

"This is Sally, your new mother."

say? Before he could think of anything to say, Sally hugged him. And Abe looked into one of the kindest faces he had ever seen. She handed Abe two books he had never read before: *Robinson Crusoe* and *Arabian Nights*. So this was how God answered his prayers. Sally was a thousand times better than anything he asked for.

Now Abe remembered his mother saying how kind the widow Sally Johnston was. Tom had certainly remembered.

Sally didn't come empty-handed. Abe helped Tom unload a chest of drawers, a table, some chairs, a box of clothing, a box of bedding, and many kitchen utensils. Tom built the second bedstead for the girls. Abe and John would sleep in the loft.

The new family celebrated the birth of Jesus. Sally roasted a turkey Tom shot, stuffed with roots and nuts the children had gathered in the forest.

One of the kindest faces he had ever seen

When Sally saw the bounty from Sarah's labor in the garden, she gave her a special hug. She cried, "Sarah has put up peas, turnips, beets, radishes, onions—and look at all the potatoes. What treasures!"

That was when Abe realized Sally and her children must have had a rough time, too. All the food he took for granted was treasure to them. In the Dutch oven in the fireplace, Sally baked johnnycakes made from cornmeal, water, and butter. They had syrup from sugar maples. They ate on pewter dishes. Abe felt like he was being born into something special again.

But Abe wouldn't rest until the promise was kept that he had made to his real mother as she was dying. He wrote Preacher Elkin in Kentucky. And when the preacher finally came to Indiana to visit a son, he went with the Lincolns to Nancy's grave. Abe was sure his mother heard Preacher Elkin's eulogy.

He went with the Lincolns to Nancy's grave.

After that, Abe didn't feel guilty for being so happy with his new mother. He was sure it was God's plan.

In the forest, Abe was handling an ax like a man. His long arms delivered such a powerful stroke that he buried the ax deeper into the wood than most men. One neighbor, hearing how fast the trees fell, thought there were several men working back in the rough. No, said Tom, it was only Abe. And now John helped Abe by stacking brush against trees.

Abe told story after story to John.

And John had stories to tell. He didn't have the kind of stories Abe craved, like the story that there was a new state west of Indiana called Illinois. But John had seen some mighty strange characters come and go in Elizabethtown. After all, he had lived only one block from the Hardin County courthouse. His favorite story was about the circus that came to town. Each time he told

One neighbor thought there were
several men working.

it, the elephant got bigger, and the lion roared louder, and the trained seal got smarter.

Abe put down his ax and sighed. "Of course, John, you know we have real bears, wolves, and panthers prowling loose right here in this forest."

John's voice was dry. "I do hear thrashing around our cabin at night." He laughed nervously. "I bet it's just the hounds."

Abe was serious. "A panther jumped the Bowers boy and girl a few years ago."

John gulped. "A panther?"

Abe said, "A panther is a hermit of an animal. It doesn't hang around roads and trails during the day." He gave John a stern look. "Just don't take any shortcuts through the forest."

"I'll remember that." John frowned, probably wondering if Abe was trying to scare him.

Abe should have let the forest speak for itself.

"I'll remember that."

A huge black form appeared from out of nowhere. It sounded taller than the trees. The bear sniffed the air, smelled the sweat of boys, and thundered back into the brush.

By 1821 when Abe was twelve, the Lincolns and their neighbors had been clearing land and planting corn for five years. The area opened up just as Abe had imagined it years earlier. Once, Abe felt the Lincolns were isolated. Now, within one mile of the Lincoln cabin were seven other cabins. Abe sat down one day and scratched a mark in the yellow soil for every child in those seven cabins.

He whistled. "Forty young folks! And that doesn't include the five of us."

Church had been held for many years but never in a special building. It was time to build a regular church structure. And who was better qualified to supervise the construction than the best carpenter in the county: Tom Lincoln. So he and neighbors

"Forty young folks!"

built a solid church twenty-six feet by thirty feet. Tom and Sally were official members.

The children went to the church every Sunday, too. But in those days it was not the custom to make them official members. Men and women became members when they got married like Elizabeth did that same year when she married Dennis Hanks. She and Dennis lived in a cabin one mile east of the Lincolns.

Abe became a sexton in the church. He ordered supplies and kept records. As he swept the floor, he would remember the persuasion in Preacher Elkin's voice and his gestures. Every Sunday morning he listened to a sermon, too. He got in the habit of preaching a sermon himself Sunday afternoon.

If Abe was still preaching to John and Matilda on Monday, Tom would notice no one was working and say, "Abe must be on the stump again." And Tom would remind

He got in the habit of preaching a sermon himself.

Abe and his audience the heavenly Father wished them to earn their daily bread.

Abe got in the habit of taking a book with him everywhere. It was as natural as grabbing an apple. Every moment he took a break from work, he read. He treasured one new book written by Ben Franklin about himself. Franklin detailed how he improved himself by setting goals for each day and at the end of the day reviewed how well he succeeded. Abe understood Franklin's ambition perfectly. Abe had a burning desire to improve himself. He loved the woods, but he didn't want to spend a lifetime cutting down trees. And he knew farming was not for him, as important as it was to raise food for folks to eat.

A second book thrilled him even more. It told the life of George Washington. Abe had never known such a sense of duty—other than the saints in the Bible. Here was a man who lived only a few years before Abe

Abe had a burning desire to improve himself.

was born. He was a man of action, but he showed such moral perfection that Abe was astounded. Washington would forever be Abe's ideal American. Abe couldn't hear the word "patriot" without thinking of George Washington. And the fact that Washington believed it was his duty to carry out God's plan confirmed his perfection for Abe.

In the yellow soil, Abe scratched the words: "Good boys who to their books apply will all be great to me by and by." Abe began to think how governments worked. He began to see why man-made laws were necessary in addition to God's command-ments in the Bible. The Bible didn't say exactly how folks paid for a school. It didn't say how folks should determine whether a man accused of a crime was innocent or guilty. Abe knew man-made laws fell short of being perfect. Otherwise, white folks wouldn't own black slaves. How did that happen? He

Washington would forever be Abe's
ideal American.

burned to know. Tom told him a man named Henry Clay from Kentucky persuaded folks to accept the "Missouri Compromise." That meant the new state of Missouri would permit slaves, but no new states north of a certain line would allow slaves. When Abe talked to John about it, John just shook his head. Why talk about such complicated things? John just wanted to talk about the elephants.

Years passed. Sarah got married. Now she was a neighbor. Abe visited courtrooms whenever he could. Folks were puzzled by the gangly young giant. What would become of him? He was a sexton in the church. He could split rails faster than anyone else. He could wrestle anyone to the ground. He talked about things nobody but a lawyer or a teacher could understand. But he didn't seem cut out for doing anything in particular.

And then, once again, tragedy struck.

Years passed.

Abe couldn't fritter his life away.

5

MOVING ON

Sadness overwhelmed Abe again. Sarah, the sweet girl who had been sister, brother, and mother to Abe, died giving birth to a baby. Abe wanted to lash out at something with his sinewy, ax-wielding arms—but he could do nothing except pray Sarah was with Jesus in heaven.

Friend Matt Gentry lost his mind. One moment Matt was fine. The next moment he was babbling, lost somewhere beyond reach. Abe waited for Matt to get better. But he didn't get better. It seemed to Abe as if by not being able to decide what to do in life, he was waiting around until something bad happened to him, too. Abe couldn't fritter his life away. Tom urged him to try other things.

Abe tried ferrying folks across the Ohio River. Allen Gentry offered Abe a different job. Allen was going to pilot a flatboat of corn and pork all the way to New Orleans. Abe accepted the offer. Tom had taken a flatboat to New Orleans himself—before Sarah was born. Maybe Abe would get married when he got back. He could hardly imagine any girl who would be interested in such a strange young man as himself.

The flatboat drifted downriver into even warmer, wetter air. While tied to shore one night near Baton Rouge, the flatboat was attacked by thieves. Abe and Allen could have jumped in the river and saved themselves, but they refused to surrender the cargo. The thieves were shocked to see a towering fury leaping about in the moonlight—a fury who broke bones with a thunderous whacking ax handle. The attackers fled, thankful to be

A towering fury leaping about in the moonlight

alive. And Abe thanked God to be alive.

The trip to New Orleans became a bad dream to Abe. He saw slaves auctioned. He saw white men poke fingers into black people as if they were livestock. New Orleans seemed thousands of years old, with sin everywhere. He could not wait to get home again. But what would he do with his life when he got back home? He would turn twenty years old on the way back to Indiana on a steamboat. All the way on the Mississippi River to Cairo, Abe prayed. All the way up the Ohio River to Troy in Indiana, he prayed. And he noticed the boat seemed to go in every direction on the looping rivers yet stayed on a relentless course from New Orleans to Troy.

The Gentrys liked Abe. He worked in their store after he got back. It would have been hard to find a better clerk than Abe. He was a true pioneer, so he knew what folks needed. And he was so strong he could lift a

Abe knew what folks needed.

keg full of nails into a wagon. He could read. He knew how to work with numbers. He could keep records. He was honest.

And more than one newcomer was startled enough to blurt, "A giant!" Abe now towered over six feet four inches tall and weighed over two hundred lean-muscled pounds.

Working in the store was to Abe's liking, too. It seemed like folks hadn't stopped talking politics since the national election the year before. Andrew Jackson, the great hero of the War of 1812, ran against President John Quincy Adams. Jackson, calling himself a Democrat, won the election. Abe loved to hear folks talk politics.

Abe felt he could prosper as a clerk, too. Had God answered his prayers? He still lived with his father, but that wasn't unusual for a man his age. The law even said he had to give his earnings to his father until he turned twenty-one. Not that Tom needed Abe's

Abe loved to hear folks talk politics.

money. Tom Lincoln had prospered from his dozen years in Indiana. He owned one hundred hogs. He harvested many acres of corn. He started building a house for Sally that no one would call a cabin.

And then Sally's sons-in-law did something that turned the Lincolns' world upside down.

Squire Hall, the husband of Matilda, and Dennis Hanks, the husband of Elizabeth, announced they were moving west—to the state of Illinois. Sally couldn't bear being separated from her daughters. Abe suddenly discovered Tom and Sally were going to Illinois, too.

Abe went along. Of course, they moved in the winter. They traveled in two wagons. The trip was two hundred miles over frozen mud and ice-covered streams. But the long, cold journey in wagons gave Abe time to think. He was grown now. It was time for him to fly from the nest. As always, he prayed that

It was time for him to fly from the nest.

God would let him do what was right. The three families stopped in central Illinois, just west of Decatur. Once again, Tom and Abe built a cabin plus corrals and a shed for the livestock.

Abe was not happy that year of 1830. He felt more out of place than ever. He didn't even have his clerking job now. He didn't want to spend his life always clearing new land, always plowing new soil. Winter came again. And it was the kind of winter that ices the land only once in a hundred years. After a blizzard dumped deep snow, the temperature never got above zero for two months!

"Who can withstand God's icy blast?" said Abe to Tom and Sally. The verse from Psalm 147 never seemed truer.

The winter was very hard on the new-comers because they didn't have large stores of food. But they survived. And by the time

"Who can withstand God's icy blast?"

spring thawed, everyone was anxious to get outside and work. Abe was so desperate to get some business, he was talked into piloting a flatboat of some goods to New Orleans again. On the way down to the Sangamon River, the flatboat ran aground for awhile at a village called New Salem. Months later, after Abe sold the corn and pork in New Orleans, he returned to Tom and Sally to say farewell. Then Abe headed for the village of New Salem. He was twenty-two and on his own at last.

He clerked in New Salem. He was so good at it, most folks quickly came to respect him. But New Salem was not like living on a farm. Rough men lived in villages. Jack Armstrong, the leader of the Clary Grove gang, challenged the newcomer to wrestle. But Armstrong was no match for a giant who had labored on the farm and in the forest almost every waking hour of his life.

He was twenty-two and on his own at last.

Jack Armstrong was a good loser. Abe was nothing like the roughnecks Jack knew. Abe didn't drink alcohol. He didn't smoke tobacco. But Abe did know how to poke fun at himself. He did tell jokes. He did have a story for every situation. He never lied. And he was a wizard at figuring things out—practical things, too. Abe made a friend for life in Jack Armstrong.

New Salem was different from the farm in another way, too. Men met to debate each other. They called themselves "free-thinkers," and Abe quickly found they thought they were free to think and say anything. Abe was shocked. It was the first time he had ever heard men question out loud whether Jesus was God. They wondered if Adam really did sin—and, if he did sin, did Jesus really pay for that sin? They wondered why God would allow death and pain in the world if He was

They questioned everything.

good. They questioned everything.

It wasn't as if Abe hadn't asked these questions. He had. Before he could read, the true answers to his questions came from his mother's lips. And after he could read, he found the true answers himself in the Bible. Abe realized that as much as he hated their attitude about Jesus, he had asked similar questions. So, if he denied these free-thinkers the right to speak out, he would be a hypocrite.

Maybe he could change some of their minds. He could not have done that to men who kept their doubts secret and pretended to believe in Jesus. Some of the men snickered at Abe. Did this backwoods roughneck who just whipped Jack Armstrong in the dusty street think he could debate educated men like a schoolmaster and a doctor?

But Abe knew the Bible by heart, and he could remember verses to advance his arguments. He especially liked to make the point

He could remember verses to
advance his arguments.

that the souls of all folks could be saved. No one was picked ahead of time to go to hell. He believed God had a plan for everyone, but folks still had to make their own choices to be saved.

He raised his arms toward the ceiling and quoted Saint Paul in 1 Corinthians 15:22: "'For as in Adam all die, even so in Christ shall all be made alive.'"

The free-thinkers argued with Abe. And Abe countered their arguments with reasoned arguments from the Bible. Their challenge was actually strengthening his spiritual armor. After awhile, Abe could tell the men were amazed that a roughneck like him had such power to reason and persuade. He worried about being too proud of himself. After all, he had God's Word to help him.

After one debate the doctor admitted, "You know, Abe, I really do believe Jesus is God."

"I really do believe Jesus is God."

Abe was surprised. "Why, you just argued hot and heavy in a debate that there is no God at all."

The doctor said, "I just like to take different sides in a debate. It helps me think things out better."

Abe replied, "I see debating is a powerful way of turning a subject inside and out." The truth was that Abe had always done that. He debated within himself.

The doctor said, "Abe, you're very good at speaking, but you still need more practice."

"Practice for what?" Abe sensed something very big was happening to him.

"Practice for what?"

"Do you want me to run for the legislature?"

6

RUNNING FOR THE LEGISLATURE

The doctor put his hand on Abe's shoulder.

"Abe," he said. "Folks, educated and uneducated, want a righteous, God-fearing man to represent their needs in the state legislature—the group of men who make the laws in Illinois. The people decide which man that is going to be with their votes. So a man has to know how to speak to them. A man has to convince them that he is the right man. And I think you might be that right man, Abe."

Abe was astounded. "Do you want me to run for the legislature?"

"Yes, I do, Abe."

The legislature? Abe, a man of the people? Abe mumbled, "It can't hurt me too much to try."

The doctor said, "Abe, you have more than the skill to debate. You have the courage of a believer who knows he is serving God by serving men and women."

The more Abe thought about it, the more eager he got. It was almost too good to be true. He hadn't lived in New Salem one year yet, and he was going to run for Illinois legislature. Maybe he would amount to something.

He thought of a plan to get elected, too.

He practiced his speech in the store, "Friends, I know a thing or two about rivers." He tucked his thumbs under imaginary suspenders. "I've been busy boating over the Sangamon River measuring depths and plotting them on maps I made. New Salem has a great future for river commerce. I want you to vote for me because I can offer you something that the other candidates can't offer you—a plan for prosperity." Abe raised

It was almost too good to be true.

his hands to the ceiling and went up on his toes.

Jack Armstrong rushed in. "Come on, Abe. A rider is here with a message from the governor!"

"What is going on?" Abe loped out the door. He found himself out in the street with dozens of other men.

The rider shouted, "Chief Black Hawk is on the warpath! Up in northern Illinois. We need men to fight!"

Fight! War! Abe couldn't believe his ears. He had never seen an Indian who was really living in the wild like an Indian. Tom told him how his father—Abe's grandpappy Abraham—was shot dead by an Indian right in front of Tom. Uncle Mord told the same story. But it didn't seem real to Abe. Besides, Abe knew Indians had been cheated by white men. Maybe as much as black folks.

"Chief Black Hawk is on the warpath!"

Abe argued with himself. Indians had been wronged. But could he stand by and do nothing while innocent settlers were killed? And he knew some white men who hated Indians. What if only that kind of man volunteered to fight? Indian women and children might be murdered.

Abe volunteered.

He had to borrow a horse. He rode hard to join sixty men gathered at a village called Richland. There was a real army officer there standing behind stacks of muskets. The officer barked, "Who is your captain?"

Jack Armstrong yelled, "I intend to come back alive! I want Abe Lincoln for a captain! Abe can whip anybody."

Abe was stunned. How could he lead men into war? He was relieved when another man yelled, "I want Bill Kirkpatrick for captain!"

Men surged toward Abe and Kirkpatrick.

"I want Abe Lincoln for a captain!"

Three times as many men surrounded Abe. "That settles it," cried the Army officer. "Abe Lincoln here is captain of this company of mounted volunteers. Get your muskets and ride north, men."

Abe had never been so proud. He had been "elected" the leader of sixty men. He remembered the Bible. Pride was dangerous. He kept that thought in his head as the company rode north to find Black Hawk.

Abe never saw Chief Black Hawk. But he learned about brave men who volunteered for such hardship. He learned what an officer has to do to keep order. His company seemed always one camp away from the fight. He knew that because they arrived the next day to bury the dead. The sight of the dead men haunted him.

Abe reenlisted twice anyway. Once he saved the life of a friendly Indian who was about to be killed by some soldiers.

He saved the life of a friendly Indian.

When the war was over, Abe felt like he had served with honor. He had been called to duty, and he went. He didn't have to shoot another man. He accepted that fate as God's plan.

He returned to New Salem three weeks before the election. He found out his job as a clerk was gone. The man who owned the store was gone, too. Abe didn't have time to worry. He campaigned hard. He showed his charts of the Sangamon River and rattled off figures. But he lost the election.

The doctor said, "Don't be bitter, Abe."

Abe wasn't bitter. He figured God didn't think he was ready to be a lawmaker in the legislature. He knew the voters didn't think he was ready. Abe studied law all the harder. But he had to earn a living, too. He didn't have his clerk's job.

A man offered him a chance to be his

He campaigned hard.

partner in a general store. He jumped at the chance. He used the one hundred and twenty-five dollars he received for his service in the Mounted Volunteers. But Abe's partner was reckless. The business borrowed more and more money. Finally, no one would loan them more money. The store closed. Abe had debts to pay off. He had failed at business. He was only twenty-three and deep in debt.

He still had a good reputation. For the next two years, he earned his living any way he could. He taught himself how to survey and earned money that way. He worked as the postmaster. He clerked in several stores. He wrote simple contracts for folks. He never lost his sense of humor. And he never lost the conviction that God had a plan for him.

Abe was a fearless storyteller around other men. But he drew inside his shell around women. He felt more than ever that he was

He never lost the conviction that
God had a plan for him.

too uneducated, too uncultured, too awkward, and too ugly. He was twenty-five years old now. He wanted a wife, but he couldn't act natural around women. He froze up. He liked Ann Rutledge enough to actually approach her and speak to her. But he learned her heart belonged to another man, even though that man had gone away from New Salem. Ann said she would never give up hope.

In two short years Abe had failed as a politician and a businessman. Would he also fail ever to win a woman's heart? Abe knew the Bible. The saints failed, too—many times. Suffering made a man stronger.

So he ran for the Illinois legislature again.

He called himself a Whig this time because Henry Clay of Kentucky was a Whig. Tom Lincoln told Abe years before that Henry Clay was a man to admire: Clay was against slavery. Clay was for a strong

Suffering made a man stronger.

nation. Abe liked Clay, too. Abe was more relaxed running for election this time. He failed once. And he would probably fail this time, too. So he told jokes. He had no elaborate plan for the Sangamon River.

And he won the election.

"Abe," said the doctor. "You won the election because folks know you will do what is right."

In no time at all, Abe found himself among eight hundred people living in Vandalia, the state capital of Illinois. Again he threw himself into a new situation, nervous about being unprepared and unworthy. He bought his first suit. But he still felt like a gawky, shaggy colt in the midst of prancing, shiny thoroughbreds.

John Stuart had just been elected for the second time. John liked the modest giant from New Salem who could tell stories. He

"Folks know you will do what is right."

took Abe around Vandalia with him. That was wonderful for Abe, who felt so unsure of himself in "fine" company. Stuart knew exactly how to act in every social situation. Abe studied his every move and learned fast. And he learned something else. Many of the lawyers in the state capital had taught themselves law and passed the examination to get a law license. Now Abe knew he had been right in studying law by himself. He studied law all the harder.

Within two years, Abe passed the law examination. He was a real lawyer. As if to remind Abe life is fragile and unpredictable, Ann Rutledge got a fever and died. She never married.

Abe was reelected. Illinois moved its state capital to Springfield. Abe roomed there with merchant Josh Speed, who soon became his close friend. Abe opened a law office with

He was a real lawyer.

John Stuart. He got reelected again in 1838. He was successful in every way but two. He still owed money in New Salem. And he wanted a wife—even if the Bible did assure him it was no disgrace not to have a wife. He prayed for God's will to be done.

At a party in December 1839, John Stuart introduced Abe to his cousin Mary Todd. She was all the things Abe feared most in a woman. She was so tiny he gawked down at the part in her fawn brown hair. He felt like Goliath. She had a turned-up nose and a sharp chin. She was very pretty. He felt uglier than ever. She was perky. Her ivory skin flushed pink as she laughed. He felt like a slow, lumbering bear. She was from a very rich family in Kentucky. Could he ever tell such a lady he grew up in a crowded one-room cabin?

She smiled, "I'm a Whig, too, Mr. Lincoln."

"I'm a Whig, too, Mr. Lincoln."

Abe couldn't believe such a pretty lady knew politics at all. But he would be polite. "Why is that, Miss Todd?"

"Why, I've been a Whig ever since I met Henry Clay."

"Henry Clay!" He was amazed.

"Mr. Clay is a friend of my father's." Mary Todd gave Abe a look that pierced his heart like an arrow. There was no mistaking what her look meant!

A look that pierced his heart like an arrow

They seemed to be meant for each other.

7

MARY TODD

Mary Todd actually liked him!

Abe thought he might actually like her, too. As Mary brightly talked politics, which Abe loved, she became more and more precious in his eyes. Yes, he liked her very much.

They were so unlike each other, and yet they seemed meant for each other. They saw each other often. They became engaged to be married. Marriage would have been soon if Mary's sister hadn't opposed it. Her sister's objections were so true that they hurt Abe. He was ten years older than Mary. Worst of all, he still owed money. He couldn't buy Mary the fine things she was used to having.

Abe crumbled under his doubts. He broke off the engagement. He slipped into a deep depression some folks called the blues.

He asked God, "How could I ever be good enough for such a fine lady?"

Abe was soon to learn God's plan for us can be very complicated. Abe's friend, Josh Speed, who had moved to Kentucky, was going through the same doubts before he married his sweetheart, Fanny. Abe visited him. Abe could counsel someone else's fears with cool, calm logic.

Josh's mother knew Abe was having problems, too. She gave Abe a beautiful white Bible. "This really is the best cure for your blues, Abe."

By the time the visit was over, Josh was cured. Abe confessed to Josh, "I believe God made me an instrument of bringing Fanny and you together. . . ."

He didn't tell Josh he was cured of the blues, too, because he wasn't sure he could make things right with Mary. He had humiliated her when he broke the engagement.

He had humiliated her when he
broke the engagement.

He visited Mary to ask for forgiveness. Mary was wonderful about it. They agreed to stay friends. Mary wrote letters to a newspaper poking fun at one of Abe's political rivals. Politics in those days could erupt into more than a battle of words—Abe's friend John Stuart and Stephen Douglas debated each other once with their fists.

Abe's political rival erupted, too. After he saw the letters to the newspaper, he challenged Abe to a duel. Abe could have said Mary wrote the letters. But he took the blame. He figured he could talk his way out of a duel with an apology. He couldn't. It seemed like a bad dream.

Abe got to pick the place and the weapons. He sent details to his rival. They would meet in the woods along the Mississippi River near St. Louis. Each would fight with the kind of long flat sword used by soldiers in the cavalry. The two duelists had to stay

He challenged Abe to a duel.

always within a rectangle ten feet by twelve feet. Abe's friends thought his choice of weapons was a joke meant to make his rival see how foolish they were both acting.

His rival didn't think it was a joke. He showed up with two swords at the edge of the great river. Abe arrived, too. Friends of both duelists managed to talk Abe's rival out of dueling only at the last second.

If any of Abe's friends had ever seen him swing an ax, they would have known he wasn't joking about using swords. Not one man in a thousand could withstand one of Abe's colossal strokes. He would have split the man like a pine log. Abe shuddered to think what might have happened. He was so ashamed that he would never talk about it again. He promised God he would grin and walk away from a fight the rest of his life—even if he didn't feel like grinning.

He was so ashamed.

Mary was thrilled. She didn't know Abe was ashamed. He hid it. She thought Abe was very brave to protect her. That bizarre incident brought them back together.

Abe and Mary married in November 1842. Etched inside Mary's wedding band were the words "Love Is Eternal."

The next years were busy, look-straight-ahead years of an ambitious man's life. Abe continued to build his political reputation. But he didn't run for legislature again. He had to get out of debt. He "rode the circuit" which meant he was a lawyer who rode out to take cases from folks in villages and rural areas. He was gone six months out of the year. But it was the surest honest way Abe knew to make money fast.

The first years were very difficult for Mary. Her sister had been right. The Mary who once wore the fanciest clothes could now afford nothing fancy. The Mary who

Abe and Mary married in November 1842.

once lived in a mansion now lived above a tavern. Son Bobby was born. He was a rowdy boy. When Abe came back from the circuit, he would comfort Mary. Then he would have to go out and work harder.

Finally, there was a light at the end of the tunnel. Abe was completely out of debt. They bought a fine, white, two-story frame house in downtown Springfield. Abe was very proud of Mary. She had endured the hardship. Bobby and their next son, Eddie, had a nice fenced-in yard where they could play.

Abe took young lawyer Billy Herndon into his law practice. Abe was setting the stage for a new phase of his career. He was planning to run for the U.S. House of Representatives the next year. That meant he and Mary would have to live in Washington, D.C. That meant Billy Herndon had to keep their law practice alive until Abe got back to Springfield.

They bought a fine, white, two-story frame house.

Mary didn't think much of Billy. He was cocky. He was a chatterbox who thought he could figure everybody out. He was wild, too, preferring the tavern to church. He griped about some of Abe's habits. His complaints got back to Mary. Billy didn't like the way Abe came in and read newspapers out loud every morning. Billy didn't like the way Bobby and Eddie came in and roughhoused in their law office.

Abe knew all of that about Billy, too. But he knew something else. Billy was completely loyal to him. Maybe Billy complained. But no one else could complain about Abe in front of Billy. Billy would challenge them on the spot.

Abe forgave Billy's faults. And Billy forgave Abe his faults. They loved each other like brothers. Abe knew he would be leaving his law practice in faithful hands if he won the election.

Abe forgave Billy's faults.

He won the election. Abe and his family left for Washington, D.C., in January 1848. About half of the 227 members of the House of Representatives belonged to the Democratic political party. The other half belonged to the Whig party. The president was Democrat James Polk. Polk had waged war against Mexico for two years. Some Whigs like Abe thought this was really a war to get more land and extend slavery—because the Missouri Compromise arranged by Henry Clay allowed new states to the south to have slavery. Of course, at the time of the compromise, Henry Clay didn't think there would ever be any new states to the south. The war with Mexico would change all that.

Abe took a strong stand against the war.

He expected the other Whigs to back him up. But they didn't.

One Whig told him, "Why make the slavery people mad? Let's just hope nothing bad happens."

Abe took a strong stand against the war.

Abe had spoken out against slavery before. Now he was going to do something about it. He was going to introduce a bill that would phase out slavery in Washington, D.C., if Congress would vote in favor of his bill. He figured that would be a small start toward solving a monstrous problem.

Another Whig found out about his plan. He asked Abe, "Have you lost your senses? Don't you know that bill will make the slavery people furious?"

Abe was disappointed in his fellow Whigs once again. But he campaigned hard for Zachary Taylor, the Whig candidate for president in the 1848 election. Abe was meeting other powerful people in the Whig party, too.

They found out how capable he was. But after Taylor won the election, Abe found out what they really thought of him. After every

"That bill will make the slavery people furious."

presidential election, the new president appointed hundreds of people to judgeships, commissions, and government agencies. Abe gave the new president, Taylor, a modest list of qualified people from Illinois. Not one person on his list was appointed.

Abe soon found out President Taylor and other Whig leaders thought he was too pushy. He was too outspoken. Why irritate the Democrats and slave owners? There could be a war between the free states and slave states. No one wanted war.

The leading Whigs had lots of experience. Abe thought it over long and hard. His final conclusion made his blood run cold: Unless reasonable people solved the slavery problem soon, there would be a war anyway. The entire United States, such a promising young nation founded on such wonderful ideals of freedom, might go up in flames. He was overwhelmed with sadness.

The entire United States. . .might go up in flames.

What was Abe supposed to do? The others in his own Whig political party refused to listen to him. He prayed for God's help.

After that, for some reason he could think of nothing but Mary. Her father had recently died. She had gone home to Kentucky for awhile. She had to force herself to return. She didn't like Washington, D.C. She thought the people were snobs. In spite of her own rich family, Mary had never been a snob. What other rich young lady would have openly embraced a rough country lawyer like Abe Lincoln?

Abe's heart ached. Mary had endured hardship for him and the boys. Just when they moved into a nice house in Springfield and Mary was her bubbly self again, Abe yanked her away from it. Now his sweet little Mary was unhappy again. God must be telling him to fix that.

One evening after they put the boys to bed, Abe said, "Mary, we need to make a powerful big decision."

"Mary, we need to make a powerful big decision."

Eddie, not yet four years old, died.

8

RACE FOR THE PRESIDENCY

Abe put his huge paw over Mary's tiny hand, "I'm thinking about getting out of politics."

"Are you sure you want to do that?" Her voice betrayed how happy she was to hear that news.

"Why don't we go back to Springfield after my term is over?"

Mary perked up. "Maybe little Eddie would get better. He's been so sick here in Washington, D.C."

And they did return to Springfield. Abe plunged into his law practice with his loyal partner Billy Herndon. Mary loved her big house. But their joy was short lived. Eddie, not yet four years old, died. Mary sunk into the depths of despair. She was touched to see a poem in the local newspaper entitled,

"Little Eddie":

The angel of Death was hovering nigh
And the lovely boy was called to die.
Bright is the home to him now given
For of such is the Kingdom of Heaven.

The newspaper didn't reveal who wrote the poem. But Mary knew who wrote it. Abe wrote it. He was sure Eddie was in heaven. He had to make sure Mary knew it, too.

Mary began to feel better. When Mary found out she was going to have another baby, both she and Abe were sure the baby was God's gift.

Willie was born in December 1850.

About the same time, Abe found out that his father, Tom, was deathly sick. Abe had drifted apart from his father. He couldn't resolve whatever difference he had with his

Abe found out that his father was deathly sick.

father, and he wouldn't talk about it. That's the way Abe was with a problem he couldn't solve. He didn't complain. He didn't gossip. He did what the Bible said; he prayed, and he hoped.

He wrote his stepbrother, John, and urged him to tell his father, Tom, to trust "our great, and good, and merciful Maker" and "if it is to be his lot to go now, he will soon have a joyous meeting with the many loved ones gone before. . . ."

One month later Abe's father died.

Death seemed to pull Abe closer to God. More and more of his loved ones were in God's Paradise. Abe accepted God's dominion with all his heart and mind.

He told a preacher at the time, "I examine the issues of life and death as rigorously as I examine any issue in a courtroom. I always conclude that divine authority and inspiration

Abe accepted God's dominion with all his heart.

of the Bible are absolute certainties."

The next years were golden. In 1853, baby Tom was born. He wiggled like a little tadpole. Abe always called him Tad. Bobby was now almost ten and Willie was three. The house was noisy. The boys were healthy. Mary was happy.

Abe practiced law, which he loved. His image as a skilled lawyer with a great sense of humor was set in these happy, relaxed years. Abe had thousands of stories he could tell to make a point. Some were funny and some were not. He didn't make up stories. He collected them. He was a masterful storyteller who never seemed to forget even one line of a story after he heard it.

He had the Bible memorized, too. It was due to his habit of always reading aloud. He felt by using the two senses of hearing and seeing instead of just one sense of seeing, he

The boys were healthy. Mary was happy.

could remember almost anything he read. He could quote by heart all the Psalms, entire chapters of Isaiah, and almost all of the New Testament. He used verses from the Bible to make points, too. And his favorite method of persuasion he learned from the Bible. Abe knew Jesus told parables because most folks remembered entertaining stories much longer than they remembered preaching.

Abe might have spent the rest of his life practicing law in Springfield if he hadn't read one morning in his newspaper about Stephen Douglas running for reelection to the U. S. Senate in 1858.

"Billy!" Abe turned a stunned face to his law partner. "It says here Douglas wants every state to vote whether it wants slavery! Even the states where black people are now free!" Abe groaned. "The problem of slavery just won't go away! It's going to get worse!"

"The problem of slavery just won't go away!"

Billy sighed. "You're the only man in Illinois who can beat Stephen Douglas."

"I don't want to go back to Washington, D.C. . . ." Abe paused. "But what choice do I have now?"

The race for the position of Illinois Senator wouldn't have attracted much attention in earlier years. But Douglas had become a national figure. He had personally destroyed the Missouri Compromise in 1854 when he devilishly pushed through a change in the law that allowed any state to adopt slavery. He was the man who spoke for slavery. He was a powerful speaker, too, so gifted he could make decent folks think slavery was all right. There was only one way to prevent that.

Abe said to Billy, "I'll debate him."

"That rascal is too smart to debate you."

The old Whig party had disintegrated over slavery. A new political party called the

Douglas had become a national figure.

Republican Party had formed against slavery. At their convention, Abe gave a speech that used the Savior's own words, "A house divided against itself cannot stand." Abe added, "I believe this government cannot endure, permanently half slave and half free."

His speech was published in newspapers all over Illinois and even in New York. Some editors were so impressed they published the entire speech as a small book.

When Douglas heard this new Republican Party nominated Abe Lincoln as their candidate for the Senate seat from Illinois, he muttered, "I'll have my hands full now. Abe is the best stump speaker in the west."

Only Mary Todd Lincoln was unhappier than Douglas. But Mary knew politics. She knew this race was much bigger than just a Senate race. It was slavery against freedom. It might make Abe a national figure.

It was slavery against freedom.

Abe showed up at the first rally for Douglas. Douglas was amused. He even invited Abe up on the platform. Abe spoke to the same crowd the next day. Abe destroyed everything Douglas had said.

At the next rally for Douglas, Abe was there again. The next day he gave his speech, ripping apart Douglas's speech. Douglas was no longer amused.

Abe kept following Douglas around Illinois, blasting apart his opponent's speeches. Newspaper reporters soon realized that both he and Douglas were magnificent speakers. The New York newspaper said, "Illinois is the most interesting political battleground in the United States."

Douglas finally realized Abe had out-smarted him. By always speaking last, Abe was hammering the last nail in every time. What could he do about it?

Abe offered a suggestion. "Debate me on the same day."

Douglas was no longer amused.

And Douglas was trapped.

They agreed to travel around the state to have a total of seven debates. Mary was thrilled now. She wished Abe good luck and blurted, "Now I know you'll be president someday, Abe."

"President!" Abe was amazed. He could only laugh.

Abe prayed for God's help. He would speak the truth during the debates, whether that was politically smart or not. He would urge folks to honor the Declaration of Independence: All men are created equal.

Douglas created fear. Did folks want blacks flooding into Illinois? Did they want blacks marrying their daughters? Did they want blacks riding in the same carriages? Eating in the same inns? In spite of Douglas's treachery, Abe got 190,000 votes and Douglas got 176,000 votes. But the senator wasn't elected by popular vote. The

"President!" He could only laugh.

newly elected Illinois state representatives voted for the senator. And Democrats outnumbered Republicans fifty-four to forty-six.

Abe lost the election!

But both men now were national figures. Both were seen—even in the east—as the best spokesmen their political parties had to offer. Two years later these two men got the nominations from their parties to run for president. But to show how divided the country was over slavery, two more political parties formed. Four men would be on the ballot for president.

It was the same debate all over again. Abe campaigned hard for president and made his position as plain and honest as he could. He was like Henry Clay. He hated slavery and would not allow any states to leave the Union!

On election day, Abe hung around the telegraph office in Springfield to hear some early results. He was winning the popular

Abe hung around the telegraph office.

vote for president. But he had won the popular vote before. Would he lose once again because the rules were strange? Each state was allotted a certain number of electoral votes, according to how many people lived in that state. But the winner of the popular vote in that state got all the electoral votes whether he won the popular vote by one vote or 100,000 votes! So, even in the national election, it was possible to win the popular vote and lose the election anyway.

Abe walked back to wait with Mary at their home. In 1860, it took a very long time to total up all the votes around the nation.

Abe thanked God for his chance. How many men got to run for president? Now he would just have to wait and see God's plan.

Would God decide Abe should fail again?

Mary said, "You should grow a beard, Abe."

Would God decide Abe should fail again?

"Why? I've never had a beard in my whole life. I'm fifty-one years old, Mary."

She smiled. "A beard will make the new president look so dignified."

Abe laughed. "I will grow a beard. God knows I need all the help I can get." Abe could always laugh at himself. When some folks called him a gorilla, Abe just laughed and said, "I'm a bit smarter, I hope."

There was a knock on the door. The minute they saw Billy Herndon's face, Abe and Mary knew the answer. . . .

Abe and Mary knew the answer. . . .

"Howdy-do, Mr. President!"

9

WAR!

A smile almost split Billy's face into two halves. He yelled, "Howdy-do, Mr. President!"

Giant Abe and tiny Mary danced a jig. The three boys whooped and hollered. Mary was even cordial to Billy Herndon. Abe fell into deep silence. The days ahead would be very dangerous. The slave states knew Abe was going to be very tough on slavery. They might strike quickly.

In early 1861, Abe stood on the platform at the back of a passenger train, saying farewell to his good friends in Springfield. His words were very sad. "I now leave, not knowing when or whether ever I may return, with a task before me greater than that which rested upon [George] Washington. Without the assistance of that Divine Being who ever attended him, I cannot succeed. With that assistance I cannot fail."

That summed it up completely. God would decide.

All over the nation, men were drifting apart, silently taking sides. The slave states attracted many good men—men Abe knew. These men chose to defend their land and their families. Abe was very saddened by that. In making that choice, they were defending a terrible evil.

Abe was sworn in as President on March 4, 1861. He hardly had time to help Mary and the three boys get settled in the White House, the mansion for the President and his family in Washington, D.C. The slave states struck quickly. Calling themselves the Confederacy, their army attacked the United States Army at Fort Sumter in South Carolina on April 12. The war had begun!

The war had begun!

Two days later Fort Sumter surrendered to the Confederates. Abe's heart ached when he got the reports of how many men had been killed. He mourned the men on both sides. This was a terrible national problem that men like himself had failed to solve. Now young men were solving the problem with their blood.

The tone of the war soon became obvious. Abe's United States Army, now called the Union Army, had vastly superior resources and numbers of men. The Confederacy had vastly superior officers. The main Union generals were timid. Abe felt like King Saul. South of Washington, D. C., there was Goliath in the person of brilliant General Robert E. Lee, standing out in the open every day, laughing and taunting the Union Army. Where was Abe's David?

In July, Abe proclaimed a national day for fasting and repenting sins. He said,

Goliath in the person of General Robert E. Lee

"It is fit and becoming in all people, at all times, to acknowledge and revere the Supreme Government of God. . .to confess and deplore their sins and transgressions in the full conviction that the fear of the Lord is the beginning of wisdom."

Cynical politicians were stunned. Who was this new president in the White House?

Abe waited and waited for a Union victory. People of the Union became upset with him. Why couldn't the Union Army fight? One of Abe's own advisors grumbled sarcastically, "Our Union Army is dug in and watching the enemy as fast as it can."

Influential people began to tell Abe to give up and let the Confederacy go its own way. The Confederacy was perfectly willing to have a standoff. Lee and his generals were brilliant at defense. If the Confederates held out long enough, all the people in the Union might finally say, "Stop. That's enough."

Influential people began to tell Abe to give up.

Abe was heard to say, "I am a humble instrument in the hands of our heavenly Father. He permits the war to go on for some wise purpose of His own, mysterious and unknown to us. . . ." Again, the cynics shook their heads.

Suddenly, son Willie died. Mary became bedridden because she was grieving so hard. Abe prayed hard. He felt like only his faith kept him from losing his mind. How much suffering could he and Mary bear?

Word drifted in of some small Union victories along the Mississippi River. A general named Ulysses S. Grant seemed to be responsible.

"What kind of general is this Ulysses S. Grant?" asked Abe.

His advisors shrugged. "He wasn't even in the Army when the war started. He has the reputation of being unreliable."

That was a polite way of saying Grant

"What kind of general is this Ulysses S. Grant?"

drank too much alcohol. Abe thought about it. He despised the effects of too much alcohol. But he considered alcoholics sick people, not evil people. Besides, people could change. Maybe Grant didn't have a drinking problem anymore. He would wait to see if this "unreliable" General Grant had any more success.

Grant did have more success. His Union Army was moving down the Mississippi, winning battle after battle. Grant was cutting the Confederacy in two!

Abe thanked God. He issued a proclamation of thanksgiving: "It is right to recognize and confess the presence of the Almighty Father. . .[to] invoke the influence of His Holy Spirit to subdue the anger, which had produced and so long sustained a needless and cruel rebellion. . . ."

Wise people in the Union began to understand Abe. God was the master of history. Abe was his instrument. Never had an

Grant was cutting the Confederacy in two!

American politician stated it so plainly.

There were really two wars now. The war in the west was being won by the Union Army under Grant's relentless offensive tactics. The war in the east was being won by the Confederate Army under Lee's clever defensive tactics.

Suddenly General Lee was no longer on the defensive. He moved his Confederate Army north into the Union state of Pennsylvania. Abe tried to think like Lee. What was he doing? Lee must think the Confederacy was in trouble. Grant was capturing the west. If Lee could now lead the Confederates north right smack into the Union and win a big battle in the east, the Union might lose heart. Abe had to admit Lee was brilliant.

In a meeting with his closest advisors, Abe said, "We are not doing enough. God will help our Union Army drive Lee out of Pennsylvania, and we will declare the slaves

"God will help our Union Army. . . ."

in the rebellious states to be free." His advisors were stunned. Some said that was a terrible mistake.

But Abe prepared his Emancipation Proclamation. On September 12, 1862, he proclaimed that on the next New Year's Day the slaves of the rebellious states were to be set free. On January 1, 1863, the president's proclamation took effect.

In July, Lee struck at Gettysburg in Pennsylvania. It was a bloody battle. Commanders used tactics from the old musket days. But their soldiers were armed with modern rifles. The slaughter was horrible. The Union prevailed. Lee retreated back to the slave states. Almost the same day, Grant won another great battle. He captured Vicksburg, a fortress along the Mississippi River long considered impossible to conquer. The Union controlled the west!

He declared all slaves free!

In November, Abe appeared at the Gettysburg battlefield with a speech of a mere 268 words. He began, "Four score and seven years ago, our fathers brought forth on this continent, a new nation conceived in liberty. . ." And he concluded with, "We here highly resolve that these dead shall not have died in vain, that this nation, under God, shall have a new birth of freedom, and that government of the people, by the people, for the people, shall not perish from the earth."

Abe knew the Bible by heart. He knew sinful nations did perish. Some newspapers thought his speech was trivial because it was so short, but several recognized it as a masterpiece.

Back in Washington, D.C., Abe got a mild disease similar to chicken pox. He joked, "At last, I have something I can give everyone."

Abe rarely lost his sense of humor, even

"Four score and seven years ago. . ."

through those terrible days. Humor helped him cope with the constant heartbreak of war. More than one person observed Abe was the saddest looking man they had ever seen—until they heard him joke. Then a smile transformed his face into radiant joy.

But in the beginning of 1864, the war in the east was once again bogged down. Abe simply had no general in the east who could fight. He prayed. The answer was obvious. Like Saul, Abe had his David. Abe must let him fight.

He said to his advisors, "I don't care what people say about Grant. The man fights."

He put Grant in charge of the entire Union Army: the most awesome military force ever assembled by mankind, over two hundred thousand men armed to the teeth with modern rifles and heavy artillery pieces.

The outcome seemed inevitable. But Abe

"I don't care what people say about Grant."

was not jubilant. He knew what this meant. The two great generals of the war now opposed each other in the east. Losses on both sides would be staggering. It was heartbreaking to think about how terrible it would be.

And suddenly the outcome was not inevitable at all. Abe had to get reelected president in 1864.

The two armies were deadlocked, slaughtering each other. The people of the Union were sick of the war and the bloodbath. The man running against Abe was none other than McClellan, one of the Union generals in the east Abe had fired—a very weak, indecisive man who couldn't fight!

McClellan confirmed it. He said if he was president, he would stop the war right away—the Confederacy could come back in the Union and keep their slaves!

Abe found out that men in his own

The man running against Abe was none other than McClellan!

Republican Party were plotting to find a Republican candidate other than Abe. They didn't think Abe had a chance of being reelected.

Never in his worst dreams did Abe think the whole struggle might end up resolving nothing. He went down on his knees. Surely God would not let this happen now.

Surely God would not let this happen now.

"I have no time for quarrels."

10

END OF THE STRUGGLE

Abe's great struggle to free the slaves seemed doomed. Abe knew God was never wrong. What was happening?

He had prayed so many times, "Oh, please, God, give me the wisdom to know what you want me to do." Had Abe made a mistake? Had he not understood God's wishes?

He just had to continue to do what he thought was right. He began to plan how he might persuade likely president McClellan to carry through with the struggle.

Mary asked, "How can you even talk to that weakling? He failed you time and time again."

"I have no time for quarrels. There's too much to do."

But in his heart Abe knew Mary was right.

McClellan would fail. He had failed Abe before—again and again.

If only Grant could defeat Lee soon. But it wasn't likely. Lee seemed determined to fight to the last man. After all, Lee knew McClellan was the answer to the Confederacy's prayers.

Abe prayed, too. It was September 1864.

Eleven-year-old Tad burst into Abe's office. "General Sherman has taken Atlanta!"

Far away from the Grant-Lee struggle in the east, the Union general Sherman had captured the great rail center of the Confederacy in the south. It was an awful blow to the Confederacy.

There was hope for the Union yet. Now if only Grant's army could finish off Lee's army. But Lee's army fought on doggedly. Lee knew exactly what was at stake: If Lincoln was not reelected, McClellan would let the slave states keep their slaves—the

"General Sherman has taken Atlanta!"

Confederacy would win after all!

The presidential election in early November crept closer and closer. It was now the middle of October.

Abe stared at his office door. *If only dear little Tad would fling that door open again and hop in with the good news. Oh, please, God. . .*

The door was flung open!

Tad yelled, "General Sheridan has routed Jubal Early! We've captured the Shenandoah Valley!"

Once again the Union had scored a giant success away from the long, bloody battle between Grant and Lee. The Shenandoah Valley in Virginia was vital to the Confederacy. Its fertile soil was a major source of their food.

"Thank God," said Abe. It was all Abe needed to say.

The people of the Union now saw an end to the struggle. They believed in Abe back in 1860. They sometimes lost faith in him. But

"Thank God."

now in 1864 they believed in Abe again.

The election results trickled in.

Abe remembered the election four years earlier. So much had happened since then. He truly felt he had become an instrument of God. And he was at peace while he waited. He had done what he thought God wanted. He hadn't been lazy about it as if God would just give him answers. He had devoted his entire heart and soul to winning the war.

Abe won 55 percent of the popular vote and won almost all the electoral votes. Once again, Abe was elected president of the United States.

The struggle to free the slaves and pre-serve the Union was as good as done. And Abe was in God's cosmic hands.

Abe was very tired. The fatigue seemed to settle in now and weigh him down. Abe almost seemed to shrink. If he had been a young man, he would have bounced up and

Once again, Abe was elected president of the
United States.

looked toward his next struggle. But he knew this struggle was his last one.

Abe was sworn in as president a second time. In a speech full of quotes from the Bible, he said, "The judgments of the Lord are true and righteous all together. With malice toward none; with charity for all; with firmness in the right, as God gives us to see the right, let us strive on to finish the work we are in. . . ."

In early April of 1865, Abe had a dream. He told Mary and some close friends about it. He dreamed he heard sobbing. He began wandering through the White House. He saw soldiers guarding a coffin. Abe asked a soldier, "Who is the dead man in that coffin?" The soldier answered, "Sir, it's the president. He was murdered by a crazy man."

"Oh no!" gasped Mary.

Mary and their close friends were very sad. Abe seemed genuinely in touch with God.

Abe had a dream.

They knew men in the Bible got dreams from angels. Could Abe's dream come true?

But the dream was forgotten. On April 9, 1865, Abe got a telegram. Lee had surrendered to Grant. The war was over.

People celebrated wildly throughout the Union. Even people in the Confederacy were glad the war was over. They had suffered tremendously. And now they were thankful the terms of peace would be in the hands of a kind giant like Abe.

It was time to relax. On April 14, Abe took Mary to Ford's Theater in Washington, D.C., to watch a play. One of the actors was a twenty-seven-year-old weak man, too cowardly to have fought in the great struggle. He was crazy, too. He wanted to take revenge for the Confederacy. He was too crazy to know that what he wanted to do would cause his own Confederacy untold suffering.

John Wilkes Booth sneaked up behind

The world mourned his death.

Abe and shot him in the head. Furious Union soldiers finally trapped the murderer days later hiding like a rat in a barn and shot him to death. Abe would not have approved of the soldiers shooting his murderer without a trial. But Abe was dead.

Abe Lincoln had died the morning of April 15, 1865.

The Union mourned the loss of their great leader. Wise people in the Confederacy mourned, too. When General Sherman told a Confederate general that Abe was dead, the blood drained from the general's face. He said, "The Confederacy lost the best friend we had."

The world mourned his death, too. The great Russian writer Leo Tolstoy said Abe's moral power and strength of character made him the greatest figure in world history since Bible times.